THE ITALIANS IN AMERICA

THE ITALIANS IN AMERICA

RONALD P. GROSSMAN, Ph.D.

Assistant Professor
Department of Humanities
Michigan State University

Published by
Lerner Publications Company
Minneapolis, Minnesota

...CONTENTS...

Christopher Columbus sets foot on the soil of the New World.

PART I.

The Age of Exploration
and Early Settlement

1. *The Navigators*

The Italians are relative newcomers to the United States. Their immigration took place largely after 1880. Yet, although they are among the newer immigrants to America, certain Italians are identified with American history from its earliest days.

The Italians were the great seafarers of the Middle Ages. During that period the ships of Venice and Genoa carried the bulk of Europe's trade. When in the 15th and 16th centuries, the Spanish and Portugese, and later the Dutch, French, and English, began to search for a direct route to China and India, they naturally called on the skills of Italian navigators. It was an Italian, Christopher Columbus of the city of Genoa, who set sail in 1492 under the flag of Spain on the voyage which discovered the New World.

Americo Vespucci, or, as he is sometimes called, Americus Vespucius. His accounts of the New World resulted in the public attaching his name to the recently discovered continents.

We owe our name "America" to the Italian explorer Americo Vespucci. He was born in Florence and became the chief admiral of the king of Spain. In 1499 he sailed down the coast of what is now Venezuela. Vespucci was among the first to recognize that Columbus had not reached the Far East, but had instead found a new continent. Through the popularity of an account he published of his travels, Vespucci's name came to be associated with the newly discovered territories. An early mapmaker used his name — Americo — to designate the southernmost of the two new continents. Later his name also came to be applied to the northern continent.

Another Italian explorer was Giovanni da Verrazano, who served the French king Francis I. In 1524, Verrazano explored the coast line of North America from the Carolinas to Cape Breton. On this voyage he discovered the Hudson River, which was to be the site of our greatest city. New York has named the magnificent new bridge across the entrance to its harbor the Verrazano-Narrows Bridge in his honor.

2. *The Missionaries*

Other Italians, especially those belonging to the missionary orders of the church, were among the first to explore the interior of the American continent. One was the Franciscan friar, Marcos de Niza. His name indicates that he was born in the city of Nice. Coming to the New World in 1531, Father Marcos worked among the Indians in Peru and Mexico. He was fascinated by their stories of seven wondrous cities, supposed to exist somewhere to the north. In 1539 he trekked northward, into the area of the present state of Arizona. His report of this journey stimulated the interest of the Spanish general Francisco Coronado, and thus Father Marcos served as the principal guide on the Conquistador's famous exploration of the American Southwest.

Eusebio Chino, a Jesuit priest, was another early Italian missionary. Between 1687 and his death in 1711 he established many missions in Sonora, in northern Mexico, and in Arizona. Several of these have become the sites of modern towns and cities. He also

explored and mapped the Colorado River, and was among the first to reach the Pacific coast of California. Father Eusebio established schools for the Indians at his missions, and was in a way the fore-runner of the cowboy, for it was he who first introduced cattle raising on the plains of the Southwest.

Christopher Columbus, the discoverer of America, was born about 1451 in Genoa, Italy. Convinced of the possibility of reaching the East by sailing westward from Europe, Columbus sought the aid of the King and Queen of Spain. Although a learned council scoffed at his proposal, Columbus won the support of Queen Isabella, and in 1492 he was equipped with a fleet of three vessels for the voyage. He set sail in August, and reached the West Indies in October. On returning to Spain in March 1493, he was received with great honors by Isabella and her husband, King Ferdinand. This first voyage was followed by three others, but Columbus' luck began to change. Rivals conspired against him, and he was twice arrested and brought back to Spain in chains. Although he cleared himself, his final voyage of 1502-04 ruined his health. The last years of his life were a period of constant illness and humiliation. After his death in 1506, his remains were returned to the New World for burial at the Cathedral of Santo Domingo. The Columbian series of postage stamps (p. 7 and 9), and the Columbian half dollar (below), were issued in 1892 to commemorate the 400th anniversary of the discovery of America.

Commemorative postage stamp (right), issued in honor of Giovanni da Verrazano. This Italian navigator explored the coast line of North America in 1524 for the King of France, and in the process discovered the Hudson River, the site of New York City. Notice the map showing the location of the bridge.

VERRAZANO-NARROWS BRIDGE

3. *Early Italian Settlers*

Apart from the explorers and missionaries, there were some early settlements of Italians. One colony was founded by Philip Mazzei, who had been a wine merchant in London. In 1773 he came to America and established a plantation adjacent to Thomas Jefferson's "Monticello." Here Mazzei began to cultivate grapes and olives, crops native to the Italian peninsula. During the American Revolution he was dispatched to Europe by Patrick Henry to raise money for the cause of the revolutionists. Although not entirely successful in this, Mazzei was able to furnish Jefferson, who had become the governor of Virginia, with important information about British military plans.

Another Italian who aided the colonists during the American War of Independence was Guiseppe Vigo. In the years before the war he had become the wealthiest fur trader on the western frontier. With the beginning of the struggle against England, he joined the rebels. He gave his financial support to George Rogers Clark, who was attempting to win the territory behind the Appalachian mountains from the British. Moreover, Vigo did not confine his assistance to money, but became an active participant in the struggle. The city of Vincennes was the key to the frontier territories; if the Americans could take it, they would win control of the region. Vigo was asked by General Clark to scout out the situation. Convincing the British that he was only a fur trader and neutral in the struggle, Vigo was able to enter the city. He made an estimate of the strength of the garrison, and he also discovered that the citizens of the city were in favor of the Americans. On receiving this information, Clark went into action. His forces took the city, and thus at one stroke more than doubled the size of the infant American republic.

Giacomo Beltrami was an Italian-American frontiersman of a slightly later date. He came to the New World in 1823, went west, and explored the Minnesota territory. This vast territory had just been added to the United States by the Louisiana Purchase. Beltrami is credited by some authorities as being the first European to reach the source of the great Mississippi River.

4. *Political Exiles of the 1840's*

In the 19th century Italy was still divided into many little principalities. Much of the Italian peninsula was under the control of outside powers, such as Austria. All through the course of the century Italian patriots worked for the expulsion of the foreigners, and the unification of their country. Each time they failed, the revolutionaries had to go into exile; many of them came to the United States. In this way a small colony of Italians developed in New York City. There the exiles established the first Italian-American newspaper, *L'Eco d'Italia,* in order to keep up with events in their homeland. They also set up the "Italian Guard," a military organization to train young men for the continuing struggle in Italy.

The flow of Italian patriots to America was especially heavy after the failure of the great uprising of 1848. Many of these exiles took service in the United States Army during the Civil War. It is estimated that over 200 Italian-Americans served as officers during that conflict. One of them, L. W. Tinelli, organized a regiment of foreign-born soldiers. He named it the "Garibaldi Guard," in honor of the famous Italian revolutionary. The regiment had a distinguished war record. It fought at the battles of Bull Run, Harper's Ferry, and Gettysburg, and was present when General Grant received Lee's final surrender.

PART II.

The Era of Mass Migration

1. *The Reasons for Immigration*

The United States underwent a remarkable change during the last years of the 19th century and the first decades of the 20th. During this period new sources of power, such as petroleum and natural gas, were developed. The invention of the dynamo in 1867 made the use of electricity practical. The development of the internal combustion engine in the 1880's promised to revolutionize transportation. These innovations opened up whole new industries, and new commercial ventures began to transform the economy. As late as 1890 the United States was primarily an agricultural country, with 42 percent of its labor force engaged in farming. Increasingly, however, at the close of the century the focus of the American economy began to shift to industry. New factories and mills springing up in every city required a never ending supply of manpower. The Italians, along with other new immigrant groups, provided the labor to run the machinery.

Most of the Italians who came to the United States were from the southern parts of the peninsula, Calabria and Naples. Others were from the island of Sicily. These were the agricultural areas of Italy, and the poorest districts. The south of Italy has always been poorer than the north, whose industry expanded rapidly in the last years of the 19th century. Few northerners emigrated to America;

Immigrants on an Atlantic Liner, 1906. The first two decades of the 20th century was the great era of Italian migration to the United States. In one year alone, over 300,000 Italians came to American shores. Many were brought over by labor contractors, called *padrones*, who often advanced passage money to whole ship loads of potential workers.

they were needed at home to staff the Italian factories. The south was different. Centuries of continuous farming had exhausted the soil, and the majority of the peasants lived in a state of never ending poverty. These Italians were to welcome the promise offered by the New World.

Up to this point the government of Italy had frowned on the emigration of their citizens. The rulers of the peninsula considered that emigration would rob them of the talents of the best of their subjects. They did everything in their power to discourage it. Now, however, they reversed themselves. During the last quarter of the

14

19th century the population of the peninsula grew tremendously. Between 1871 and 1905 it increased by 25 percent. The Italian government came to see emigration as a way of relieving over-crowding. Restrictions were removed, and emigration became a kind of "safety valve," a means of reducing the number of hungry mouths, and thus nipping political unrest in the bud.

2. Periods of Migration and the Size of the Immigrant Community

Even among the newer groups attracted by the expansion of American industry the Italians arrived rather late. The peak of Italian immigration was not reached until well into the 20th century. Once they found American shores, however, the Italians came in ever increasing numbers. In one year alone Italy sent over 300,000 immigrants — more than the whole population of the city of Venice. Between 1890 and 1950 over 4,700,000 Italians immigrated to the United States. The census of 1940 showed that the 4,594,780 Italian-Americans constituted 13 percent of the foreign stock (individuals born abroad, or with a parent born abroad) of the country. This made the Italians the second largest national grouping, exceeded only slightly by the German-Americans.

Immigration from Italy by Decades

1831-40	2,000
1841-50	2,000
1851-60	9,000
1861-70	12,000
1871-80	56,000
1881-90	307,000
1891-1900	652,000
1901-10	2,046,000
1911-20	1,110,000
1921-30	455,000
1931-40	68,000
1941-50	57,000

Italian-American Population

	Total	Foreign Born
1900 . . .	738,513	483,963
1910 . . .	2,114,715	1,343,070
1920 . . .	3,361,200	1,610,109
1930 . . .	4,546,877	1,790,424
1940 . . .	4,594,780	1,623,580
1950 . . .	4,570,550	1,427,145

Italian Populations of Major Cities

(According to latest figures available — 1950)

		Percentage of Total
Akron, Ohio	6,860	2½
Baltimore, Md.	23,666	2½
Boston, Mass.	78,650	10
Bridgeport, Conn.	21,387	13½
Buffalo, N.Y.	51,311	9
Chicago, Illinois	171,549	5
Cincinnati, Ohio	6,743	1
Cleveland, Ohio	47,970	5
Denver, Colo.	8,318	2
Detroit, Michigan	68,076	4
Elizabeth, N. J.	11,043	10
Hartford, Conn.	22,146	12½
Houston, Texas	5,453	1
Jersey City, N. J.	39,344	13
Kansas City, Mo.	7,929	2
Los Angeles, Calif.	47,240	2½
Milwaukee, Wisc.	12,411	2
Minneapolis-St. Paul, Minn.	6,529	1
Newark, N. J.	69,418	16
New Haven, Conn.	36,133	22
New Orleans, La.	21,340	4
New York, N.Y.	1,028,980	13
Oakland, Calif.	14,427	4
Omaha, Nebr.	6,761	3
Paterson, N. J.	28,322	20
Philadelphia, Penn.	163,926	6
Pittsburgh, Penn.	45,101	7
Portland, Oregon	5,859	1½
Providence, R.I.	47,960	19
Rochester, N.Y.	52,100	16
St. Louis, Mo.	19,488	2
San Antonio, Texas	1,994	½
San Diego, Calif.	6,445	2
San Francisco, Calif.	53,011	7
Scranton, Penn.	9,356	8
Seattle, Wash.	7,040	1½
Somerville, Mass.	15,520	15
Springfield, Mass.	12,606	8
Syracuse, N.Y.	22,503	10
Toledo, Ohio	2,183	1
Trenton, N. J.	18,271	14
Washington, D.C.	13,592	2
Waterbury, Conn.	23,588	23
Worcester, Mass.	12,470	6
Yonkers, N.Y.	18,706	12
Youngstown, Ohio	17,449	10

Italian Population by States

(According to latest figures available — 1950)

		Percentage of Total (no figure = less than ½%)
Alabama	5,786	...
Arizona	5,495	1
Arkansas	2,410	...
California	201,045	2
Colorado	43,682	3½
Connecticut	239,150	12
Delaware	11,181	3½
Florida	26,992	1
Georgia	2,938	...
Idaho	2,153	½
Illinois	260,926	3
Indiana	17,718	½
Iowa	9,158	½
Kansas	4,219	...
Kentucky	4,353	...
Louisiana	37,718	1½
Maine	7,118	1
Maryland	36,432	1½
Massachusetts	329,428	7
Michigan	114,502	2
Minnesota	15,446	½
Mississippi	4,907	...
Missouri	34,795	1½
Montana	4,932	1
Nebraska	5,922	½
Nevada	5,285	3
New Hampshire	4,821	1
New Jersey	507,295	10
New Mexico	3,274	½
New York	1,191,530	8
North Carolina	3,193	...
North Dakota	391	...
Ohio	172,368	2
Oklahoma	3,165	...
Oregon	10,181	½
Pennsylvania	555,069	5½
Rhode Island	89,600	11
South Carolina	1,455	...
South Dakota	862	...
Tennessee	5,597	...
Texas	23,289	...
Utah	5,705	1
Vermont	6,196	1½
Virginia	10,412	...
Washington	22,681	1
West Virginia	27,007	1
Wisconsin	32,468	1
Wyoming	2,803	1

Typical views in the crowded immigrant sections of the Lower East Side of New York City. The street was the place in which to buy and sell. It is still the same in many parts of the world today. These scenes took place around 1900. We see the fish market *(above)* and the pushcart vendors with their many types of merchandise—clothing, groceries, fruits, vegetables and dry goods *(below)*.

The first two decades of the 20th century were the great years of Italian immigration. Although the number of arrivals had been increasing steadily since the 1880's, the pace of immigration quickened after the turn of the century. Between 1901-10 over two million Italians entered the country; from 1911-20, over one million.

This massive immigration of the Italians and other new nationalities frightened many of the older Americans. After the first World War they began to call for restrictions, and in the 1920's Congress established the Quota System. By this legislation annual immigration quotas were set for each nation. These were fixed at a percentage of the numbers of each nationality living in the United States in 1890. Obviously, the system favored the older groups over the newer nationalities. As a result of the introduction of the quotas, Italian immigration declined through the 1930's and even more in subsequent decades. Under the quota system, which has recently been abolished, only some 5,000 Italians annually were allowed to enter the country.

3. *Areas of Settlement*

Coming to the United States usually involved a complete change in the immigrant's way of life. Newcomers had once been able to find cheap, or even free, land to farm in our western territories. By the close of the 19th century, when the Italians began to come in significant numbers, the frontier was gone and the free land virtually all taken up.

Some few Italians were able to find agricultural work in their new homeland. They established truck farms in New England, the Great Lakes region, and Florida, and supplied the cities of these areas with fresh fruits and vegetables. Others, skilled in the cultivation of grapes, founded vineyards in California. Some Sicilians were able to find a place for themselves in the fishing industries on the Gulf and Pacific coasts. In San Francisco the Italians came to dominate the wharfs and boats.

Only a small fraction of the newcomers were able to continue

Mulberry Street. As a result of massive Italian immigration many American cities came to have a "Little Italy," a whole section occupied almost entirely by Italians. One such was Mulberry Street, on the Lower East Side of New York City.

their traditional occupations. The majority had to find such work as they could. Most could not speak the language of their new home. Many had only a hazy idea of what life was like in America. The immigrants were most often brought over by labor contractors. Frequently the contractors were Italians, called *padrones,* who had lived for a few years in the New World and discovered the manpower needs of American industry. They would return to their native villages and enlist others to come over. By advancing passage money, the contractors would bring in whole shiploads of potential laborers.

Many of these early immigrants intended to stay in America only for a short time. They planned to work hard, save their money, and then return to their villages and purchase land with their earnings. Through the first decade of the 20th century, thousands of immigrants would leave America each year to return to Italy. In 1908, for example, 160,000 sailed back home, about half the number of Italians who entered the United States that year.

A bit later, the *padrones'* recruits began to think of America as a new and permanent home. The man who had left his family behind saved his earnings for their passage to the New World. The immigrants made homes for themselves in the industrial cities of the United States. They came to New York, Boston, and to other cities where factories offered work. The Italians became one of the most urban of American groups. The census of 1940 found that 88 percent of Italian-Americans were city dwellers. Geographically this has concentrated the Italians in the heavily urbanized states of the Northeastern seaboard. They became significant minorities in Connecticut, Massachusetts, New Jersey, New York, Pennsylvania, and Rhode Island. Smaller groups are found in California, Colorado, Delaware, Illinois, Nevada, and Ohio.

PART III.

The Character of the Italian Immigrant and His Experiences

1. *Leonard Covello's Story*

Leonard Covello, a noted Italian-American educator, recounted the days of the great migration in his autobiography. He remembers his father going off to the United States at the turn of the century. The rest of the family remained behind. Leonard anxiously asked each visitor from America for news of his father, until that day when the family's passage money finally arrived.

The Covello family went to live in the East Harlem section of New York. He and his brothers attended a "Soup School." It was so called because the children were given a bowl of soup each day at noon. The charity workers who ran the school knew how difficult life was for the newcomers. Leonard, in spite of all difficulties, worked hard at his lessons. From the "Soup School" he went on to Columbia University, from which he graduated Phi Beta Kappa.

He became a teacher, and then the principal of the Benjamin Franklin High School in East Harlem. For 22 years he devoted himself to the sons and daughters of the groups who succeeded the Italians in the neighborhood. Working with the Negroes, the Puerto Ricans, and the others who came to live in East Harlem, he demonstrated the possibilities of using the schools to enrich the lives of all the members of the community, the adults as well as the children.

2. *"Little Italy"*

Like the Covellos, other immigrant families were attracted to the American industrial centers. Many cities and towns came to have a "Little Italy," a whole neighborhood inhabited almost entirely by Italians. Often the "Little Italy" was divided into sections, each occupied by immigrants from the same village or district in the old country. Leonard Covello lived on 112th Street, which in those days was almost a colony of the town of Avigliano in southern Italy.

The neighborhoods into which the Italians crowded were run-down, and sometimes already slums. These were areas of the city where earlier immigrant groups, such as the Irish and Germans, had previously lived. They had prospered in their adopted homeland and were moving out of their older neighborhoods and making homes for themselves in the newer districts of the city. As they moved out, the Italians moved in. Since these areas had already housed several generations, the Italians inherited tenements and apartments which had long since seen their best days. However, because of the magical lure of America, the "Little Italys" were quickly filled to overflowing.

3. *Hardships of Life in the New World*

In the early days of mass immigration, life in America was often disorganized. This was especially true when the men came over without their families, intending either to return to Italy, or to send later for their wives and children. In the old country the individual's life had been regulated by the strong bonds of his family and his ancestral village. In the United States these bonds were shattered.

Some immigrants did not even find permanent homes in their new country. They were forced to wander about from town to town in search of work. They would hire out for a time on the railroads, working with the gangs which maintained the tracks. When that gave out, they might join other crews mixing cement and laying down the highways which were then linking the towns of America. They would help to construct the new tall buildings which were filling out the skylines of the cities. Such migrants had little opportunity to put down roots, forced as they were to pick up and move on every few months.

Even those who had permanent work found life in the New World far different from that which they had known in Italy. They had come from a poor country and had known poverty, but life there also had its good side. Although the Italian peasant was poor, he usually owned his own home. If he drew a meager living from the soil, at least he was doing work which he knew and often loved from long experience. Above all else, Italy was the land of his fathers; he and his native land knew each other well.

Transplanted to a new and strange country, the immigrant found himself shut up in the tenements of "Little Italy." No longer did he work like his ancestors on the land. He now labored long hours at the machines in the factories or he bent his back over a pick and shovel. In Italy he had heard stories of the fortunes waiting to be made in America. In the New World, however, he discovered that a man could suddenly find himself without any work at all. The early Italian immigrant glimpsed a way of life around him which he only dimly understood.

4. *Prejudice and Discrimination*

Not only was America confusing to the immigrant. He seemed a strange creature in the eyes of his adopted countrymen. All Americans are, of course, the descendants of immigrants, but people have a convenient memory of the past. The older groups had forgotten, by the time of the Italian migration, that their ancestors had once been newcomers. They saw themselves as the true Americans; these others were "foreigners." Until the great

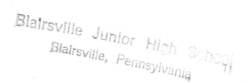

wave of immigration at the end of the 19th century, the United States had been populated by peoples of northern and western Europe who shared similar customs.

The Italians, and the other newcomers of the turn of the century, were "different." Like all Mediterraneans, the Italians were and are a marvelously expressive people. They take no pride in disguising their feelings or hiding their emotions. They love their melodic language—the tongue of Dante and Petrarch—and speak it loud and clear, and at a pace which approaches at times the speed of light. No Italian feels able to communicate with his vocal cords alone. He needs his arms and hands, his whole body, to fully express himself.

The United States Post Office issued a commemorate stamp to honor the 700th anniversary of the birth of the great Italian poet Dante in 1265.

All too often the older groups failed to appreciate the qualities of the newcomers. Looking at conditions in the Italian sections, they confused cause and effect, and concluded that the immigrants must be inferior. They judged that the Italians were condemned to heavy and unskilled labor because they were fit for no other. Stories went about of the violence and lawlessness of the Italians.

In the popular conception, "Little Italy" was a den of vice. An outsider entered only at the danger of his life. Actually, statistics show that even in the earliest days of their migration, the Italian crime rate was not significantly different from the national average. This in spite of the very great difficulties which the immigrants faced in their new home.

Forced to live in the most rundown sections of the city, and faced by the hostility of older Americans, many immigrants lost heart and chose to return to Italy. Many others retained, in spite of all, their faith in America. Pascal d'Angelo was one of these. He came to the New World with his father in the early years of this century. For years the father and son worked at whatever jobs they could find. They moved up and down the east coast and lived in a dozen and more towns and cities. Finally one day, Pascal's father announced that he was beaten. He was calling it quits and going back to his native land. He asked his son to return with him.

"I shook my head," Pascal remembered years afterwards. "Something had grown in me during my stay in America. Something was keeping me in this wonderful, perilous land where I had suffered so much and where I had so much more to suffer. Should I quit this great America without a chance to really know it? Again I shook my head. There was a lingering suspicion that somewhere I would strike the light. I could not remain in the darkness perpetually." Pascal d'Angelo's faith was not misplaced. He was to lay down his pick and shovel one day, to take up pen and paper, and become a celebrated Italian-American poet and writer.

5. *Mother Cabrini*

If many Americans failed at first to recognize the worth of their new neighbors, others were more farsighted. Pioneering social workers and reformers worked to correct the situation in "Little Italy." Furthermore, the immigrants were not for long solely dependent on the goodwill of their fellow citizens. The Italians themselves began to improve their living conditions. Most notable in this work was Mother Frances Cabrini.

Mother Frances Cabrini, founder of the Order of the Missionary Sisters of the Sacred Heart. Mother Cabrini did important social work in the early Italian communities of the United States. She was canonized in 1946, the only American citizen to be raised to sainthood by the Catholic Church.

Mother Cabrini had from an early age dreamed of doing missionary work for her church. In 1880, she founded the Missionary Sisters of the Sacred Heart, intending that they begin their mission in China and India. Pope Leo XIII, however, convinced Mother Cabrini that there was much important work to be done among the neglected immigrants in the United States. Bringing her followers to America, she began to work in the slums of Chicago. She and the sisters of her Order established schools, orphanages, and hospitals for the immigrants. Mother Cabrini, who died in 1917, was declared a saint by the Catholic Church in 1946. She was the first, and so far the only, American citizen to be accorded this high honor.

6. *Fraternal Organizations and Journals*

The immigrants came to establish their own welfare agencies and fraternal organizations. The largest of these was the *Ordine Figli d'Italia*—the Order of the Sons of Italy. This organization, founded in 1904, had at its height over 300,000 members. It was founded as a self-help society and created summer camps for children and nursing homes for the aged members of the community. In the early days, the Order conducted Americanization classes for the newest arrivals from Italy. More recently, it has established Italian language schools for the members of the second generation.

The Italians also established their own newspapers and journals. The pioneering paper was *L'Eco d'Italy*, founded back in 1849. By the decade of the 1930's, the Italian press held second place in circulation among the foreign language newspapers in New York City. The most important of the daily papers of that era was *Il Progresso Italo-Americano*.

7. *Improved Job Opportunities*

As the 20th century progressed, the Italians began to move up the social ladder. When they first came to American shores, the immigrants had little to offer but the sweat of their brows and the labor of their strong backs. In time they and their children learned the ways of their new homeland and were able to find new and better employment. In 1916 almost half of all Italian-Americans were still common laborers. By 1931 only 30 percent were still in this category. In subsequent years this figure declined further until the census of 1950 showed only 11 percent so employed.

In the 1930's the Italians began to enter in increasing numbers into the skilled job categories. They became mechanics, plasterers,

Luigi Antonini *(left)*, a noted labor leader, was First Vice-President of the International Ladies' Garment Workers Union, and the organizer of the Italian-American Labor Council. Local 89 of the Garment Workers, of which Antonini was general secretary, at one time enrolled some 37,000 Italian-speaking workers.

James C. Petrillo *(right)*, a prominent Italian-American labor leader, was the long time head of the American Federation of Musicians.

bakers, and butchers. Many turned to barbering. It is estimated that at one point 85 percent of New York's barbers were of Italian descent. Large numbers of Italian-Americans became skilled workers in the cloth trades. At one time the Italians all but monopolized the garment industry in Philadelphia. Almost a third of the garment workers in Chicago, in Boston, and in New York were of Italian origin. They became equally numerous in the textile industry of New England.

In recognition of their important place in the industry, the International Ladies' Garment Workers Union chartered an Italian speaking local in 1919. The general secretary of Local 89, which enrolled 37,000 members, was Luigi Antonini. He was also First Vice-President of the International, and organized an Italian-American Labor Council with a membership of over 300,000. As other immigrants made use of their native musical talents, the American Federation of Musicians came to be almost an Italian preserve. Its long time President was James C. Petrillo, whose immigrant father had labored at digging sewers for the city of Chicago.

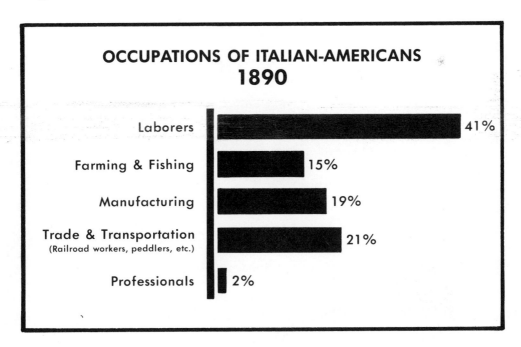

OCCUPATIONS OF ITALIAN-AMERICANS
1890

Laborers — 41%

Farming & Fishing — 15%

Manufacturing — 19%

Trade & Transportation
(Railroad workers, peddlers, etc.) — 21%

Professionals — 2%

OCCUPATIONS OF ITALIAN-AMERICANS
1950

Laborers	11%
Farming	2%
Skilled Workers	20%
Semi-Skilled Workers	28%
Services	6%
Salesmen	6%
Clerical	8%
Managerial	10%
Professionals	6%

NATIONAL AVERAGE OF OCCUPATIONS
1950

Laborers	6%
Farm	10%
Skilled	20%
Semi-Skilled	20%
Services	6%
Sales	5%
Clerical	6%
Managerial	11%
Professionals	6%

Other Italians became white collar workers, store clerks, and salesmen. As the walls of "Little Italy" broke down, the sons and daughters of immigrants began to attend colleges and universities. In increasing numbers they entered into managerial positions and the higher professions. As a result, while at the turn of the century the immigrants were almost confined to unskilled labor, by 1950 the Italian-Americans were distributed through the several employment categories in roughly the same proportions as the rest of the population.

8. *World War II*

The absorption of the immigrants into the mainstream of American life was demonstrated by their unswerving loyalty during World War II. When the dictator Benito Mussolini first came to power, some Italian-Americans championed Fascism because of their pride in the country of their ancestors. Others, however, like the labor leader Luigi Antonini, were from the outset firm opponents of totalitarianism. The dictator's cowardly attack on the helpless African nation of Ethiopia turned public opinion against him.

When the United States declared war on Italy in 1941, the most prominent Italian-American newspapers rejected Fascism and

Lt. Willibald C. Bianchi *(left),* was awarded the Medal of Honor for his bravery in personally wiping out two enemy machine-gun nests during the battle for the Philippines.

Private Frank J. Petrarca *(center),* was awarded the Medal of Honor for administering medical aid to his fellow soldiers under heavy fire during the campaign for the Solomon Islands. He was killed while trying to reach a wounded comrade who lay only twenty yards in front of the enemy lines.

Major Ralph Cheli *(right).* In August of 1943, Major Cheli was leading his squadron in an attack on a Japanese air field on New Guinea when enemy fire caused his plane to burst into flame. Instead of parachuting to safety, and at the cost of his life, Major Cheli continued to lead his formation to a successful completion of the mission.

whole-heartedly supported our government's war effort. There were still some 700,000 immigrants who had not yet taken American citizenship at the time of Pearl Harbor. This gave the Italian-Americans a greater percentage of aliens than any other group. Only a tiny fraction of this number, however, came under any suspicion of disloyalty. Less than 100 had to be interned for the duration of the conflict.

Over 400,000 Italian-Americans served the United States during the Second World War. They distinguished themselves in every branch of the armed services, and at least seven received the Congressional Medal of Honor. By a curious turn of fate, the campaign of the Fifth Army up the Italian peninsula offered many second generation Italian-Americans their first opportunity to see the towns and villages of their parents.

Sergeant Peter J. Dalessondro *(left)*. On Dec. 22, 1944 Sergeant Dalessondro's unit was subject to a heavy attack by the Germans. Rushing to a forward position, he covered the withdrawal of his men until his own ammunition was exhausted. While the enemy surrounded his position, he remained alone, hurling grenades and calling over his radio for artillery fire closer and closer to his outpost. He was last heard ordering a final barrage, saying "Okay mortars, let me have it — right on this position."

Sergeant Veto R. Bertoldo *(center)*, was awarded the Medal of Honor for defending his command post continuously for 48 hours, without relief or rest, during the campaign in France. Because of his bravery, his battalion escaped destruction. He killed 40 Germans and wounded many more.

Private Joseph J. Cicchetti *(right)*. At the cost of his life, he led a litter bearer team that rescued 14 wounded men in the face of intense Japanese fire. Although mortally wounded, he completed his final rescue and carried a comrade to safety.

Private Gino J. Merli, manning a machine gun post in Belgium in 1944, covered the withdrawal of his company from the attack of a superior enemy force, and shot down 20 Nazi soldiers. Although his post was overrun, he escaped capture by playing dead.

PART IV.

Contributions to American Life

1. *Commerce and Industry*

Through the years many once penniless immigrants worked themselves up to positions of wealth and influence. Such is the story of Generoso Pope. He began his career in his adopted homeland as a waterboy on a road gang. Coming to New York City in 1904, he went to work for a construction company, and by 1917 he was the president of the organization. Eventually he ran a vast financial empire, which included newspaper holdings as well as his construction business.

Another rags-to-riches story is that of Sebastiano Poli. His early days were spent as an organ-grinder on the streets of New Haven, Connecticut. From his first savings he purchased a small theater, then another, and still another. Eventually, he sold his chain of motion picture theaters to the Fox Movie Corporation for over 30 million dollars.

Amadeo Giannini was the son of immigrants who had come to California. At the age of 12 Amadeo went to work for a produce firm. By 19 he had worked himself up into a partnership in the business, and by 30 he was able to retire from this first career. Next he opened a small bank in San Francisco and specialized in making loans to people of limited means who could not usually find credit. By 1930 he had built this original enterprise into the

Amadeo P. Giannini, the son of Italian immigrants, was the founder of the Bank of America.

Birthplace of the Bank of America. On this site in 1904 Giannini opened his first banking office, which in those days he called the Bank of Italy.

powerful Bank of America, the largest bank in the United States, with branch offices from coast to coast. Giannini was also a leading philanthropist. When he died in 1949, he provided that much of his personal fortune should go to the University of California.

There is also the example of John F. Cuneo of Chicago. He took over a family business and built it into the Cuneo Press, the largest printing establishment in the world. Many of our leading national magazines are printed on the presses of the Cuneo plant.

Among other contemporary leaders of business and industry are Salvatore Giordano, president of the Fedders Corporation, manufacturers of air-conditioning equipment, and Jeno Paulucci, president of the Chun King Corporation, the leading processor of Chinese food.

Salvatore Giordano, president of the Fedders Corporation, leading manufacturers of air-conditioning equipment.

Jeno Paulucci, president of the Chun King Corporation.

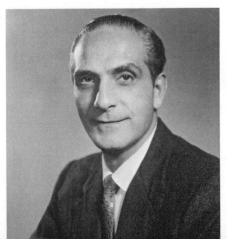

2. *Politics*

The advancement of the Italians also took place in American political life. Because of the isolation of their people, early Italian-American politicians had only limited opportunities. They had to operate as the loyal and subordinate allies of the leaders of other groups. In the 1930's Italian political leaders began to come into their own. An early example is Ferdinand Pecora who was born in Nicosia and came to the United States in 1887. By hard work and diligent study he won degrees from the City College of New York and the New York Law School. Entering political life, he served from 1918 to 1930 as the Assistant District Attorney for New York City. He was then appointed by President Roosevelt as one of the original members of the Securities and Exchange Commission, a position he held until being made an Associate Justice of the Supreme Court of New York.

FIORELLO LA GUARDIA

The first Italian-American to achieve national prominence was Fiorello La Guardia. Affectionately known as the "Little Flower," he became one of the most colorful and beloved figures on the American political scene. He was born in New York in 1882 of Italian and Jewish parents, and is thus the perfect representative of the American melting pot. While a young man La Guardia served as an interpreter at Ellis Island, through which the majority of immigrants entered the United States. At the same time he studied law in night school. He began his political career as Deputy Attorney of the State of New York, and then won election to Congress on the Republican ticket, the first Italian-American to do so.

When the United States entered the first World War, the year following his election, La Guardia immediately volunteered for the Air Corps. Serving on the Italian front, he quickly rose to major and was decorated by King Victor Emmanuel for his exploits in the air. In 1918, while he was still in military service, his district again returned him to the House of Representatives. Holding a Congressional seat almost continuously until 1932, La Guardia attracted

Fiorello La Guardia, former Mayor of New York, and the first Italian-American political figure of national prominence.

national attention by his campaign for legislation to improve the conditions of the working man.

Although he lost his Congressional seat in the Democratic landslide of 1932, La Guardia quickly bounded back. The following year he won election as mayor of New York, breaking the longtime hold of the Democrats on the city. He turned this trick twice more, in 1937 and 1941. As mayor, La Guardia endeared himself to the voters by demonstrating a very real love for the city and her citizens. His most important contribution was a program to tear down the city's slums and replace the tenements with new low-cost housing.

Even more important than the concrete monuments of his term of office was the attitude which he brought to the job. No problem was too difficult for La Guardia to tackle, no detail of government too small for his attention. He kept a helmet and raincoat in his office. Whenever the alarms signalled a major fire, he would dash out to direct "his" firemen, even if it meant keeping a whole delegation of visiting dignitaries waiting. La Guardia won himself immortality during a strike against New York's newspapers. It seemed that the children of the city would have to miss the adventures of their comic-strip heroes. Not so. The Little Flower simply read the "funnies" over the air on the city's radio station!

Vincent R. Impellitteri was born in the village of Isnello, on the island of Sicily, and became president of the New York City Council, and then mayor of the city.

Michael V. DiSalle. Mr. DiSalle's parents were emigrants from the town of Vasto, Italy. He has been a member of the Ohio legislature, the mayor of Toledo, and the governor of Ohio.

Senator John O. Pastore. Mr. Pastore was the first Italian-American to serve as the governor of a state. His political career began in the Rhode Island General Assembly, and he served successively as Assistant Attorney General, Lieutenant Governor, Governor, and Senator. He is a trustee of Brown University.

John A. Volpe, Governor of Massachusetts. His parents immigrated to America from Teamo, Italy. He was formerly the Federal Highway Administrator.

THE NEW POLITICAL SCENE

As their people came to be a sizable minority in many American cities, other Italian-Americans also won election as mayors. Angelo Rossi served as mayor of San Francisco from 1931 to 1944. Robert S. Maestri occupied that office in New Orleans between 1936 and 1946. Thomas D'Alessandro was the mayor of Baltimore in the late 40's, and Vincent Impellitteri served in New York in the 50's. Other Italians have been mayors of Cleveland, Toledo, and Youngstown, Ohio; Jersey City, Paterson, Hoboken, Orange, and Passaic, New Jersey; and New Haven, Connecticut.

Robert N. Giaimo, Congressman from Connecticut. Mr. Giaimo served in the army during World War II, and was first elected to Congress in 1958.

Dante B. Fascell, Congressman from Florida. Mr. Fascell saw World War II action in the African, Sicilian, and Italian campaigns and was first elected to Congress in 1954.

Joseph Minish, Congressman from New Jersey. Mr. Minish has been the executive secretary of the Essex County Congress of Industrial Organizations. He was first elected to Congress in 1962.

Silvio O. Conte, Congressman from Massachusetts. Mr. Conte served with the Seabees during World War II. The Massachusetts Junior Chamber of Commerce chose him as the Outstanding Young Man of 1954. Mr. Conte was first elected to Congress in 1958.

Peter Rodino, Congressman from New Jersey. Mr. Rodino served with the Military Mission to the Italian Army and was awarded the U.S. Bronze Star, and the Order of Merit and the Star of Solidarity of the Italian Republic. He was first elected to Congress in 1948.

Frank Annunzio, Congressman from Illinois. Mr. Annunzio has been the educational representative of the United Steelworkers' Union, and served as the Director of Labor of the State of Illinois. He was first elected to Congress in 1964.

Dominick V. Daniels, Congressman from New Jersey. Mr. Daniels has been a magistrate of the Jersey City Municipal Court, and the vice-chairman of the Jersey City Civil Rights Commission. He was first elected to Congress in 1958.

Joseph Vigorito, Congressman from Pennsylvania. Mr. Vigorito was formerly an Assistant Professor at Pennsylvania State University. He was first elected to Congress in 1964.

Teno Roncalio, Congressman from Wyoming. Mr. Roncalio won the Silver Star in World War II. He has been the chairman of the Wyoming Democratic State Central Committee, and was first elected to Congress in 1964.

John O. Pastore was the first Italian-American to serve as the governor of a state, occupying that office in Rhode Island from 1945 to 1950. He then won another first by being elected to the United States Senate. Michael V. Di Salle, who earlier was the mayor of Toledo, occupied the governor's mansion in Ohio between 1958 and 1963. John Furcolo served two terms in the 50's as governor of Massachusetts. The Massachusetts elections of 1964 demonstrated the important role of the Italian-Americans in that state. Both the Republican and Democratic candidates for governor, John A. Volpe and Francis Belloti, were of Italian descent.

La Guardia was followed to Congress by a dozen other Italian-Americans who served terms during the 1930's and 40's. Several representatives of Italian background were elected in 1964: Emilio Daddario and Robert Giaimo of Connecticut, Dante Fascell of Florida, Frank Annunzio of Illinois, Silvio Conte of Massachusetts, Peter Rodino, Joseph Minish, and Dominick Daniels of New Jersey, Joseph Vigorito of Pennsylvania, and Teno Roncalio of Wyoming.

Anthony J. Celebrezze, former Secretary of the Department of Health, Education and Welfare. Mr. Celebrezze was born in Anzi, in southern Italy. Like his father, he began life as a railroad track worker. He served in the Ohio senate, and was five times elected mayor of Cleveland.

Joseph A. Califano, Jr. Mr. Califano was formerly assistant to Secretary of Defense McNamara, and is now on the White House Staff of President Lyndon B. Johnson.

Michael A. Musmanno, Associate Justice of the Pennsylvania Supreme Court. Mr. Musmanno served during World War II as an aid to General Mark Clark. He served as a justice of the Nuremberg Tribunal, and on the Commission on International Rules of Judicial Procedure.

Anthony J. Celebrezze recently held the highest position of any Italian-American in the Federal branch of the government. Mr. Celebrezze, who was born in Italy, began his political career in the Ohio State Senate. After serving five terms as the mayor of Cleveland, he was appointed by President Kennedy to the Cabinet as the Secretary of the Department of Health, Education, and Welfare. Other Italians holding high positions in the federal branch include Henry L. Giordano, Commissioner of the Bureau of Narcotics, and Joseph Califano, Jr., a member of President Johnson's White House staff.

Among judges, the pioneer was Frank Angellotti who was the Chief Justice of the Supreme Court of California from 1915 to 1921. Besides Ferdinand Pecora, Felix Benvenga and Salvatore Cotillo each served on the Supreme Court of New York in the 30's. The most distinguished contemporary Italian-American jurist is Michael A. Musmanno. Mr. Musmanno served on the War Crimes Tribunal which tried the chief Nazis leaders of World War II. At present he is an Associate Justice of the Pennsylvania Supreme Court.

3. Music

Italians have always given their musical talents to America. When the Metropolitan Opera House of New York opened in 1883, one of its first conductors was Cleofante Campanini of Parma. From 1906 to 1909 he served as the associate director of the Met. Then he moved on to Chicago where he occupied the positions of conductor, director, and general manager of the Opera Association.

Also from Parma is Arturo Toscanini, the most celebrated conductor of recent times. He began as a cellist and in 1885 was touring South America with an opera troupe. One evening, when the company was playing in Rio de Janeiro, the conductor failed to show up. Toscanini mounted the podium and directed the whole opera *Aida* from memory. When he laid down his baton the audience broke into thunderous applause and Toscanini was launched on a new career.

In the United States, Toscanini first conducted at the Metropolitan in 1908, and from 1926 headed the New York Philharmonic Orchestra. Nor did he confine his activities to the recital hall. In the 1930's Toscanini began a memorable series of radio broadcasts,

ARTURO TOSCANINI

Arturo Toscanini. Mr. Toscanini, the most celebrated orchestral conductor of recent times, was born in Parma, Italy. From 1926 to 1937 he conducted the New York Philharmonic, and from 1937 until his retirement in 1954, the National Broadcasting Company Symphony Orchestra.

Enrico Caruso, the great tenor, was born in Naples. He made his American debut with the Metropolitan Opera in 1903, and was the star of that company until his death in 1920.

bringing good music into the homes of millions of average Americans. Because of the immense popularity of these broadcasts, the National Broadcasting Company created a symphony orchestra specifically for the great conductor. Toscanini headed this NBC Symphony from its birth in 1937 until his retirement in 1954. In addition to its radio performances, he took the organization on a number of tours through the United States and Latin America.

The composer Gian Carlo Menotti is another outstanding Italian-American musician. A child prodigy, Menotti composed his first opera at the age of 11. He has won acclaim in several different fields; his works have been produced over radio and television and made into motion pictures. Opera is not usually considered a popular art in the United States, as it is in Italy.

Menotti's *The Medium,* however, was a commercial success in a Broadway theater and was later made into a movie. He wrote *Amahl and the Night Visitors* for television presentation. The opera tells the story of the encounter of a poor crippled boy with the Three Kings on their journey to Bethlehem. Acclaimed at the time of its original showing in 1951, *Amahl* has become a regular feature of the Christmas season. Among other honors, he received the Pulitzer Prize in 1950 and 1954. The second was for *The Saint of Bleecker Street.* Menotti found the material for this play in the experiences of the Italian immigrants in New York.

Gian Carlo Menotti. This contemporary Italian-American composer was a child prodigy, composing his first opera at the tender age of eleven. He was twice honored with the Pulitzer Prize.

A Scene from *Amahl and the Night Visitors.* This opera by Menotti tells the story of a poor crippled boy and the Biblical Three Kings of the East. First presented over television in 1951, *Amahl* has become a regular feature of the Christmas season.

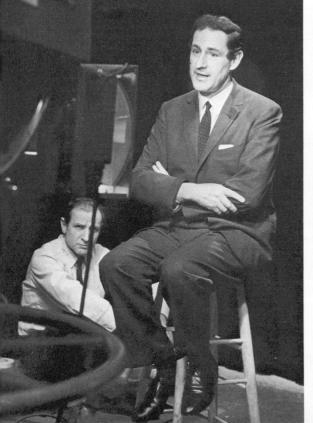

4. *The Fine Arts*

The artist Constantino Brumaldi heads the list of Italian-Americans who have distinguished themselves in the fine arts. His first important work was a group of fresco paintings at the Vatican, the home of the popes. As a young man, Brumaldi was an active Italian patriot and took part in the uprisings which swept the peninsula in 1848. That year Italian nationalists attempted to expel the Austrians from Italy and establish a free and independent nation. Failing, however, the revolutionaries had to go into exile; Brumaldi chose to come to the United States. Here he contributed his talents to the decoration of the Capitol in Washington. He designed and painted a series of murals which illustrated our country's history. Although he was over 70 when he finished that project, Brumaldi immediately took up another. He began to paint a huge frieze around the great central rotunda of the Capitol. He died before finishing the work, but a pupil, a fellow immigrant, completed his designs.

Luigi Palmi di Cesnola also combined artistic and adventurous careers. After serving with the Italian army in the Crimean war, Cesnola immigrated to America. His first service to his adopted country was as a major in the 11th New York Cavalry during the Civil War. In reward, Cesnola was named by President Lincoln to be the American consul on Cyprus. Arriving at his diplomatic post he became interested in the excavation of the historical monuments of the island. Although he had no formal training in archaeology and only limited funds, he was able to recover thousands of relics of this ancient Mediterranean civilization. When his discoveries became known, Cesnola was deluged with offers. He rejected all others when the New York Metropolitan Museum agreed to take the whole collection and maintain it intact. He then entered on still another career, becoming the Secretary and then the Director of the newly opened Metropolitan. Cesnola served as Director from 1879 until his death in 1904 and was instrumental in building up its collections and establishing an international reputation for the museum.

Piccirilli's *Fireman's Monument (above)* was erected by the city of New York in recognition of the services of her firefighters.

Attilio Piccirilli, the noted Italian-American sculptor, was born in Tuscany, Italy. His monument, *The Maine Memorial (left),* was erected in honor of the memory of the soldiers and sailors who lost their lives in the Spanish-American War.

Attilio Piccirilli, born in Tuscany and trained like his father as a sculptor, immigrated to the United States in 1888. He won a commission to design the *Maine Memorial* erected in New York's Central Park in memory of the soldiers and sailors who lost their lives in the Spanish-American War. He also created a highly unusual glass sculpture to decorate Rockefeller Center. Piccirilli took time from his own creative work to look to the training of others. For this reason he served as the president of the Leonardo Da Vinci Art School, established to provide for the artistic education of underprivileged young people.

Harry Bertoia, a leading contemporary sculptor and furniture designer. He is here shown working on preliminary studies for his modern sculpture *Sunlit Straw.*

Harry Bertoia is a contemporary Italian-American artist. Many leading architects have called on his talents. His sculptures can be seen in the General Motors Technical Center in Detroit, the Manufacturer's Trust Bank in New York City, the chapel at the Massachusetts Institute of Technology, and the Dulles Airport in Washington. Bertoia is also a noted designer of modern furniture; his famous "wire chair" has won him numerous citations. His honors include the Prix de Rome of the American Academy of Arts and Letters.

Antonio Salemme is another important contemporary Italian-American artist. Among his works is a bronze sculpture of former President Eisenhower. The piece has recently been installed in the library of Columbia University, as a gift from a group of the school's alumni.

Sunlit Straw, as seen installed in the lobby of the Northwestern National Life Insurance Company building in Minneapolis, Minnesota.

A bronze head of former President Eisenhower, the work of Antonio Salemme, another contemporary Italian-American sculptor. He was born in Gaeta, Italy. This head has recently been presented to Columbia University by a group of its alumni.

5. *Scholarship, Science, and Literature*

Italian-Americans have served on the faculties of leading colleges and universities. One of the first was Lorenzo da Ponte. A poet, he worked in Europe as a librettist for Mozart. Coming to this country in 1805, Da Ponte initiated the study of Italian at Columbia University. In recent times, Dino Bigongiari served as Head of Columbia's Italian Department, and Rodolph Altrocehi occupied a similar position at the University of California.

Henry Suzzalo was president of the University of Washington and a director of the Carnegie Foundation for the Advancement of Teaching. John T. Rettaliata is president of the Illinois Institute of Technology. He has also served as a member of the National Aeronautics and Space Council, the organization which directs the nation's space effort. Giorgio de Santilliana, a leading historian of science, has been a member of the faculty at both Harvard and the Massachusetts Institute of Technology. Fittingly, one of his books is a study of the 17th century Italian scientist Galileo.

Gaetano Salvemini, a noted historian of the French Revolution, began his career at the University of Rome. Entering politics, he won election to the Chamber of Deputies, the equivalent of our House of Representatives. There he was an outspoken enemy of the Fascists. Following Mussolini's rise to power, Professor Salvemini went into exile, and eventually joined the faculty of Harvard University.

The leading Italian-American scientist was also an exile from Mussolini's regime. Enrico Fermi, born in 1901, did his first research at the University of Rome. He was awarded the Nobel Prize for physics in 1938. An opponent of the Fascists, he took advantage of his trip to Sweden for the prize to flee Italy. Coming to the United States, Professor Fermi worked at Columbia and then at the University of Chicago. In co-operation with Leo Szilard, an immigrant from Hungary, Fermi conducted man's first controlled nuclear reaction. This experiment of 1942 led directly to the development of the atomic bomb. An annual award

Enrico Fermi (1901-1954), the distinguished physicist and Nobel Prize winner, was a refugee from Mussolini's Italy. His experiments led directly to the development of the atomic bomb. In his honor, the United States government has established an annual prize, the Atomic Energy Commission Enrico Fermi Award of $25,000 for contributions to the safe use of nuclear power.

Eugene G. Fubini, Assistant Secretary of Defense, 1963-65. Dr. Fubini directed the nation's military research program for two years. Another refugee from the Fascists, Dr. Fubini had been an associate of Fermi at the University of Rome.

for distinguished research in physics has been established by the United States government in honor of the memory of Enrico Fermi.

One of Fermi's associates in his nuclear research was Dr. Eugene G. Fubini. Fubini immigrated to America in 1939. From 1963 to 1965 he held the position of Assistant Secretary of Defense, and directed the nation's military research efforts. He left this position to become vice-president for research of the International Business Machines Corporation.

Emilio Segre was another of Fermi's associates at the University of Rome. In 1936 he discovered "technicium," the first element to be artificially created. Coming to America in 1938, Professor Segre joined the staff of the Lawrence Radiation Laboratory

Emilio Segre. Dr. Segre, who was born in Tivoli, Italy, came to the United States in 1938, and has served on the staff of the Lawrence Radiation Laboratory, and at the Los Alamos Laboratory. Dr. Segre was awarded the Nobel Prize in physics in 1959 for his research into the structure of matter.

at the University of California. During the Second World War, he was a member of the Los Alamos Laboratory, where the first atomic bomb was produced. Returning to Berkeley after the war, Dr. Segre discovered the anti-proton, and opened up the whole mysterious world of "anti-matter." He received the Nobel Prize for physics in 1959.

Bernard DeVoto is perhaps the leading man of letters produced by the Italian-American community. He began his career as a teacher at Northwestern and Harvard Universities, but soon turned to writing. From 1936 to 1938 he was editor of the *Saturday Review of Literature*. His output was astounding: he wrote novels, works of criticism, and histories. When his finances demanded it, he also wrote mystery stories under the pseudonym of "John August." His study of Mark Twain was based on a thorough examination of that writer's unpublished papers. The most controversial of DeVoto's books was *The Literary Fallacy,* in which he made a broad attack on the American authors of the 1920's. He argued that Sinclair Lewis, Hemingway, and the others of that generation had been guilty of a gross misinterpretation of the culture of their native land. Much better received was *Across the Wide Missouri,* in which DeVoto told the story of the pioneers of the American West. This work was awarded the 1948 Pulitzer Prize for History.

Paul Gallico was for 13 years the sports editor of the New York Daily News. Leaving that position in 1936, he became a free lance writer for leading magazines and newspapers. During the war he was the European correspondent of *Cosmopolitan.* Mr. Gallico is also the author of several novels, and he created the screen play for *Pride of the Yankees,* the movie biography of Lou Gehrig.

There are several prominent contemporary Italian-American poets. Henry Rago published his first work in *Poetry Magazine* at the age of 16. John Ciardi has published several volumes of poetry, is a noted literary critic, and serves as the poetry editor of the *Saturday Review.* His translations of the Italian poet Dante have won wide acclaim. Among Mr. Ciardi's honors are the Poetry Magazine Award of 1944 and the Harriet Monroe Memorial of 1955.

Max Ascoli, the editor of *The Reporter* magazine, began his career as a political scientist in Italy. He was an opponent of Mussolini, and a regular contributor to several underground anti-fascist newspapers. Because of this activity he was arrested in 1928 and prevented from taking a position on the faculty of the University of Rome. A Rockefeller Foundation fellowship allowed Mr. Ascoli to visit the United States. Deciding to remain in permanent exile, he joined the New School for Social Research in 1933, where he served as Dean of the Graduate Faculties in 1940-41. Mr. Ascoli is the author of several books, including *Intelligence in*

Politics and *The Power of Freedom.* In 1949 he founded the *Reporter* as a forum for independent thought on important contemporary problems.

6. *Cuisine*

Italians have made notable contributions to America's diet. Italian-American truck farmers introduced their fellow citizens to several vegetables which were unknown in this country but old favorites in Italy. They brought broccoli, zucchini squash, endive, and chicory to the American dining table. Other gardeners transplanted many varieties of Italian grapes to the vineyards of California. Finally, of course, there is the pizza pie. Born centuries ago in Naples, it became in the 1950's as much an American as an Italian custom.

John Ciardi. Mr. Ciardi is the poetry editor of the *Saturday Review,* and has published several volumes of his own verse.

7. Sports and the Entertainment World

Italians have also contributed to the enrichment of American life through their accomplishments in the entertainment and sporting worlds. Through the years Americans have danced to the bands of Ted Fiorito, Vincent Rose, Tony Pastor, Guy Lombardo, Lou Prima, and Ralph Marterie. Italian "crooners" include Russ Columbo, Frank Parker, Perry Como, Dean Martin, Tony Bennett, Frankie Laine, and Frank Sinatra. Among our leading comics are

Frank Sinatra has made innumerable hit records, appeared on television shows, and in many motion pictures. He won an Oscar as the "Best Supporting Actor of 1953" for his part in *From Here to Eternity.*

Guy Lombardo and his "Royal Canadians" dance band have appeared at many leading hotels and ballrooms.

Perry Como first came to prominence with the Ted Weems band, and is presently the star of his own television show.

Dean Martin, who was born Dino Crocetti, is the son of immigrant parents. With his former partner, Jerry Lewis, he appeared in some 16 movies.

Tony Bennett, the noted popular singer, has had numerous record hits, and was named by *Cash Box* magazine as the "Best Male Vocalist of 1947."

Frankie Laine's parents came to America from the village of Lo Vecchio, near Palermo, Sicily. Among his hit records are *That's My Desire* and *Mule Train*.

Lou Costello was part of the famous Bud Abbott-Lou Costello team. He began as a boxer and movie stunt man, and only later turned to comedy.

Lou Costello and Jimmy Durante. In motion pictures, Rudolph Valentino was the idol of American women in the 1920's. Vincent Edwards, Sal Mineo and Anthony Franciosa are outstanding actors of the present day. Frank Capra, the winner of three Academy Awards, has been one of Hollywood's most respected directors.

In the world of sports, Gene Sarazen won fame in golf, while Willie Mosconi is the long time champion of the pocket billiards table. In boxing, Lou Ambers was the lightweight champion in the 30's and Rocky Graziano the king of the middleweights in the late 40's.

Rudolph Valentino was the most celebrated star of the silent movie era. His birthplace was Castellaneta, Italy. He began as a landscape gardner, and rose to world fame as the star of such films as *The Sheik*, and *Blood and Sand*.

Jimmy Durante's mother was an emigrant from Salerno, Italy. Mr. Durante has brought his own distinctive brand of comedy into many leading night clubs, and has appeared on television and in motion pictures.

Henri Mancini took his first music lessons from his father, who played in a "Sons of Italy" band. He has won two Oscars for his musical compositions for films.

Gino Cappelletti, outstanding professional player with the Boston Patriots of the American Football League. He was chosen the most valuable league player in 1964, and led in scoring in 1964-65.

Anna Maria Alberghetti. Born in Pesaro, Italy, she sang for GI audiences during the Fifth Army's campaign up the peninsula. She made her American debut in Carnegie Hall at the age of 13.

Ezio Pinza was born in Rome, and first appeared at the La Scala Opera House, under Toscanini. In the United States, Mr. Pinza was a star of the Metropolitan from 1926 to 1948. He won national fame on Broadway for his role in *South Pacific*.

Rocky Marciano was born Rocco Marchegiano, and is the only undefeated heavyweight champion in the history of boxing. In 1952 he won the title from Jersey Joe Walcott, and held it until his retirement in 1956.

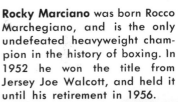

VINCE LOMBARDI

JOHN ROMANO

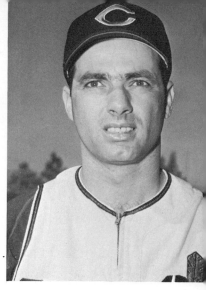

ROCKY COLAVITO

Rocky Marciano, the "Brockton Bomber" is the only unde-feated heavyweight champion in the history of the sport. In foot-ball, the most successful coach of recent years has been Vince Lombardi of the Green Bay Packers. Eddie Arcaro rode to five Kentucky Derby victories and is one of three jockeys ever to ride a total of 4,000 winners. A whole host of Italian-Americans have won fame on the baseball diamond. The Di Maggio family, who came from Sicily to the San Francisco area, sent three sons to the major leagues. The most famous, Joe — "The Clipper" — was the perennial

FRANK MALZONE

TONY CONIGLIARO

TITO FRANCONA

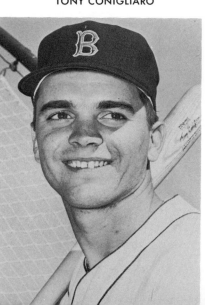

star of the New York Yankees between 1936 and 1951. One of his teammates was Phil Rizzuto, who won the American League's Most Valuable Player Award in 1950. Yogi Berra played with and managed the Yankees, while Joe Garagiolo played for the St. Louis Cardinals and has gone on to a new career as a sportscaster. Today the major leaguers include Joe Pepitone of the Yanks, John Orsino of the Orioles, John Romano of the White Sox, Rocky Colavito of the Indians, Jim Fregosi of the Angels, Frank Malzone and Tony Conigliaro of the Red Sox, Tito Francona of the Cardinals, and Jim Pagliaroni of the Pirates.

Joe DiMaggio was the star of the New York Yankees from 1936 until 1951. He appeared in nine World Series and had a lifetime batting average of .329. Joe was elected to Baseball's Hall of Fame in 1955.

JOSEPH PAUL DI MAGGIO
NEW YORK A.L. 1936 TO 1951

HIT SAFELY IN 56 CONSECUTIVE GAMES
FOR MAJOR LEAGUE RECORD 1941. HIT 2
HOME-RUNS IN ONE INNING 1936. HIT 3
HOME-RUNS IN ONE GAME (3 TIMES). HOLDS
NUMEROUS BATTING RECORDS. PLAYED IN
10 WORLD SERIES (51 GAMES) AND 11 ALL
STAR GAMES. MOST VALUABLE PLAYER
A.L. 1939, 1941, 1947.

61

Conclusion

As the list shows, Italians have distinguished themselves in all areas of American life. The immigrant of yesterday has been Americanized, while the rest of the nation has become just a little bit Italian. Today the Italian-American newspapers have to include an English section for the benefit of second and third generation readers. On the other hand, old Italian folk songs have been winners on the Hit Parade, and everybody loves a pizza.

ACKNOWLEDGEMENTS

The illustrations are reproduced through the courtesy of: p. 6, Bureau of Indian Affairs; pp. 7, 9, 10 (right), 24, Post Office Department, Division of Philately; p. 10 (left and center), the Smithsonian Institution, Division of Numismatics; pp. 14, 19, Library of Congress; p. 28 (left), International Ladies Garment Workers Union; p. 28 (right), Harris and Ewing; pp. 31, 32, 33, 42 (center), 52, United States Army; p. 35 (top left), Gabriel Moulin — S.F.; p. 35 (top right), Bank of America; p. 35 (bottom left), Fedders Corporation; p. 35 (bottom right), Blackstone-Shelburne N.Y.; pp. 37, 47, Art Commission, City of New York; p. 42 (left), Department of Health, Education and Welfare; pp. 43, 44 (left), 45 (left), 57 (top right and bottom left), 59 (top left and center, bottom center), National Broadcasting Company, Inc.; p. 44 (right), Metropolitan Opera Archives; pp. 45 (right), 56, 57 (top center), 59 (bottom left), 60 (bottom left, center, right), TV Times; pp. 48, 49 (left), Northwestern National Life Insurance Co.; p. 49 (right), Columbia University; p. 51 Los Alamos Scientific Laboratory; p. 53, Lawrence Radiation Laboratory, University of California; p. 55, *Saturday Review*; pp. 57 (top left, bottom center, bottom right), 58, Station WCCO, Minneapolis; p. 59 (top right), Boston Patriots Football Club; p. 59 (bottom right), The Ring Book Shop; p. 60 (top left), Green Bay Packers; p. 60 (top center), Chicago White Sox; p. 60 (top right), Cleveland Indians; p. 61, National Baseball Hall of Fame.

ABOUT THE AUTHOR...

DR. RONALD P. GROSSMAN was born in Chicago, and obtained his education at the University of Illinois, the Illinois Institute of Technology and the University of Chicago. In 1965, he received a Ph.D. degree in history from the University of Chicago for his doctoral thesis on *The Financing of the Crusades*. Dr. Grossman has been an Instructor in the Department of History at the University of Nebraska, and Assistant Professor in the Department of History at St. Olaf's College, Minnesota. He is now Assistant Professor in the Humanities Department at Michigan State University, and resides in East Lansing, Michigan with his wife and daughter.

The IN AMERICA *Series*

The CZECHS *and* SLOVAKS *in America*
The DUTCH *in America*
The EAST INDIANS *and* PAKISTANIS *in America*
The ENGLISH *in America*
The FRENCH *in America*
The GERMANS *in America*
The IRISH *in America*
The ITALIANS *in America*
The JAPANESE *in America*
The NEGRO *in America*
The NORWEGIANS *in America*
The SCOTS *and* SCOTCH-IRISH *in America*
The SWEDES *in America*
The FREEDOM OF THE PRESS *in America*
The FREEDOM OF SPEECH *in America*

We specialize in publishing quality books for
young people. For a complete list please write:

LERNER PUBLICATIONS COMPANY
241 First Avenue North, Minneapolis, Minnesota 55401